Improvising Bass Guitar

Early Stages

Written by
Tony Skinner

on behalf of
The Registry of Guitar Tutors

ISBN: 1-898466-31-9

A CIP record for this publication is available from the British Library.

Published in Great Britain by

Registry Mews, 11 to 13 Wilton Road, Bexhill, Sussex, TN40 1HY

Typesetting by Take Note Publishing Ltd., Lingfield, Surrey

Printed in Great Britain

For information on bass guitar exams contact

Registry RGT

Registry of Guitar Tutors

Tel: 01424 22 22 22

www.RegistryOfGuitarTutors.com

Contents

CD running order

Track 1	Tuning guide	Track 8	Reggae
Track 2	Country Rock	Track 9	Pop
Track 3	Power Ballad	Track 10	Country
Track 4	'60s Pop	Track 11	Romantic Ballad
Track 5	Rhythm 'n' Blues	Track 12	Ska
Track 6	Classic Soul Ballad	Track 13	Jazz
Track 7	Disco Funk		

Introduction

The purpose of this book is to introduce the concept of improvisation on bass guitar. Developing your skills in this area will help you gain the ability to create your own bass lines over chord progressions in a wide range of musical styles. For any bass player wishing to join a band this is an essential skill. However, this ability is often difficult to acquire unless you have someone on-hand to provide the backing chords for you to improvise over. Fortunately, the accompanying CD provides a full band backing track (minus the bass part) for all the musical examples shown within this book. By playing along with the CD you'll be able to hear how your bass lines sound in a real band setting. Use the tuning guide [CD TRACK 1] to make sure that you're fully in tune before you begin.

Bass Exams

This book is structured in line with the Registry Of Guitar Tutors bass guitar examination syllabus. It introduces the concept of improvisation at beginner level (known as Preliminary Grade) and steadily progresses through the early stages of Grades One and Two.

The book provides an ideal study aid for those preparing to take a bass guitar examination, however it is designed so that it can be used by all budding bass players whether intending to take the examination or not.

Basic technique

Right hand

1. Walk don't hop

Pick the strings by alternating between your first and second fingers (known as index and middle). Although you can hop along on one leg, it's much easier to walk using two legs. The same principle applies to bass playing – never pick the same string repeatedly with the same finger; always alternate your picking. If using a plectrum rather than fingers, make sure that you alternate between downstrokes and upstrokes to pick the strings.

2. Have a rest

To get a strong tone and maintain control over your picking you need to use rest strokes. First rest the tip of your finger on the string you wish to play. The finger should then press toward, and finally come to rest on, the adjacent lower string. Avoid any temptation to pluck out from the guitar body.

Left hand

1. Top of the tips

Fret notes by pressing with the very tips of your fingers. As fingertips are much less flabby than the pads of the fingers it's much easier to fret notes with clarity and without the need to use excess pressure.

2. On the edge

It's essential that you press at the very edge of the frets – right next to the fretwire. This minimises both buzzes and the amount of pressure required; enabling you to play with a lighter, clearer and more fluent touch.

Preliminary Grade

The first step in creating your own bass lines is to start by playing the root note of each chord. To keep things simple at this level, we have limited the range of chords to G, A, B, C, D and E. These notes are easy to locate as they occur on frets 3, 5 and 7 of the two lowest strings; these frets are normally highlighted by 'marker dots' inlaid into the fingerboard.

The diagram below shows the fingerboard of the bass guitar and the location of the notes G, A, B, C, D & E.

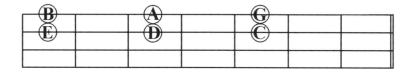

Root notes only

Using the CD, play along with the chord progressions shown on the following page. Start by listening to one verse of the sequence before you begin so that you can grasp the style, mood and tempo of the music. Listen carefully to hear when the chord changes occur. Begin to improvise by playing just the root note over each chord – e.g. on the chord of G play the note of G. Although you are only using one note within each bar you have total freedom over how many times you play that note within each bar – in other words you can create a rhythmic figure using that one note. The rhythm can be as simple or as creative as you like, as long as it suits the musical style of the track. At first it's safest to maintain the same rhythm on all chords; you can experiment with variations once you are able to play through the sequence securely.

Backing tracks

CD TRACK 2 – Country Rock

$\frac{4}{4}$ | G | C | G | C | Am | D | Em | Em ‖

CD TRACK 3 – Power Ballad

$\frac{4}{4}$ | Am | Dm | Em | Dm | G | C | Dm | Am ‖

CD TRACK 4 – '60s Pop

$\frac{4}{4}$ | C | Am | C | Am | Dm | Dm | G | G ‖

CD TRACK 5 – Rhythm 'n' Blues

$\frac{4}{4}$ | D | G | A | Bm | D | Em | A | A ‖

Root and fifth

Once you are able to play through all the sequences using root notes you can start to expand your range of improvisation by adding the fifth note of each chord. The fifth note can always be found two frets higher than the root note on the adjacent higher string. For notes on the A string, the fifth of the chord can also be played in a lower octave on the same fret as the root note, but on the adjacent lower string.

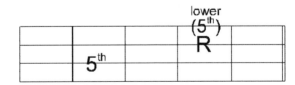

Using the CD, play along with the chord progressions again. This time experiment by occasionally adding a fifth note. At first you might like to establish a fixed bass pattern and alternate between the root and fifth in a regular way. Once you become used to incorporating the fifth note, try and improvise a little more freely and vary the way that you use the fifth on different chords. There is no need to play the fifth on every chord; as long as you play the root note you will always stay in tune. How much use you make of the fifth note is really a matter of taste and style. As an improviser it's one of the decisions that you need to make based on your interpretation of the mood and tempo of the music.

Minor / major fingering

Some chords have the letter 'm' after them. This indicates that the chord is minor rather than major. At this stage this doesn't effect what you should play over the chord. However, to prepare you for fingering patterns that you will go on to play at a later stage it is advisable to get into the habit of using the fingering illustrated below.

Major

For major chords, fret the root note with the 2nd finger and the fifth note with the 4th finger.

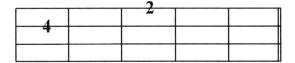

Minor

For minor chords, fret the root note with the first finger and the fifth note with the third finger.

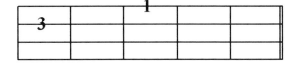

Grade One

At this level, we are still limiting the range of chords to G, A, B, C, D and E (majors or minors). These notes are easy to locate as they occur on frets 3, 5 and 7 of the two lowest strings; these frets are normally highlighted by 'marker dots' inlaid into the fingerboard. These are also the most commonly occurring chords in popular music and so it's important to gain a thorough knowledge of these chords before progressing onto lesser used chords.

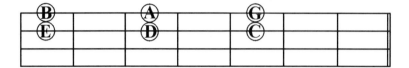

Root and fifth

Before attempting the new techniques that are introduced at this level you should be fluent in creating bass lines using the root and fifth of each chord. If you are not confident in this area you should revise the contents of the Preliminary Grade chapter before proceeding.

Root, third and fifth

By adding the third note of a chord to your improvisations you will be able to make your bass lines much more melodic. Whereas the root and fifth notes are the same whether the chord is major or minor, the third note varies depending upon whether the chord is major or minor.

With the first finger on the root note, the fourth finger on the same string should lie over the minor 3rd.

To play a major 3rd place your second finger on the root, enabling the major third to be played with the first finger on the next string up, one fret lower.

Minor 3rd & 5th

Major 3rd & 5th

Using the CD, play along with the chord progressions below. Experiment by occasionally adding a third note to your improvisation. At first you might like to establish a fixed bass pattern that uses the root, fifth and third in a regular way (remembering to alter the third depending upon whether the chord is major or minor). Once you become used to incorporating the third note, try and improvise a little more freely and vary the way that you use the third on different chords. There is no need to play the third on every chord – how much use you make of the third note is really a matter of taste and what you think best suits the musical style. Listen carefully to the backing track in order to choose an appropriate style of bass line.

Backing tracks

CD TRACK 6 – Classic Soul Ballad

$\left|\!\frac{4}{4}\right.$ A | A | D | Bm | A | E | A | A $\|$

CD TRACK 7 – Disco Funk

$\left|\!\frac{4}{4}\right.$ Em | D | C | D | C | Am | G | D $\|$

CD TRACK 8 – Reggae

$\left|\!\frac{4}{4}\right.$ Am | Em | Dm | G | Am | Em | G | Am $\|$

CD TRACK 9 – Pop

$\left|\!\frac{4}{4}\right.$ C | Am | Dm | G | Em | Am | G | G $\|$

Grade 2

At this stage it's time to expand your playing of major and minor arpeggios to all keys. The table below shows the starting points for all 12 keys. If you are not fluent in incorporating root, third and fifth notes into your bass lines (over the common chords of G, A, B, C, D and E) then you should revise the previous chapters before proceeding.

arpeggio	F♯/G♭	G	G♯/A♭	A	A♯/B♭	B	C	C♯/D♭	D	D♯/E♭	E	F
starting string	E	E	E	E	E	E	A	A	A	A	A	A
starting fret	2	3	4	5	6	7	3	4	5	6	7	8

Root, third, fifth and seventh

At this level you should begin to play seventh chords. To start with it would be sensible to restrict the use of seventh chords to the popular pitches of G, A, B, C, D and E. There are three types of seventh chord:

major 7th	(Maj7)
minor 7th	(m7)
dominant 7th	(7)

On the following pages, examples are given starting on G and C – showing the patterns for arpeggios starting on the E string and the A string respectively. For other pitches refer to the table above which details the starting string and fret for each arpeggio.

Guitarographs

The arpeggios are illustrated using the Registry Of Guitar Tutors' unique Guitarograph system.

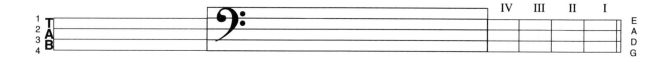

The *Guitarograph* uses a combination of tablature, traditional notation and fingerboard diagram. These are explained individually on the following pages:

(1) Tablature

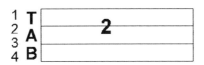

The horizontal lines represent the strings in descending order, as indicated. The numbers on the string lines refer to the frets at which the left-hand fingers should press. The above example therefore means: play on string 2 at fret 2.

(2) Bass clef notation

The lines and spaces of the bass clef indicate notes as follows:

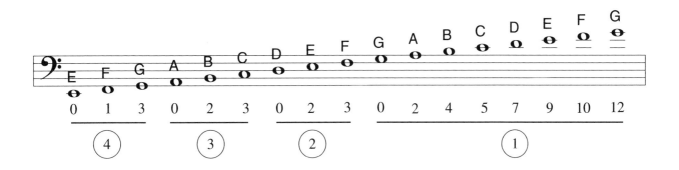

A sharp (#) before a note *raises* its pitch by a semitone, i.e. the note is played one fret higher.

A flat (♭) before a note *lowers* its pitch by a semitone, i.e. the note is played one fret lower.

In the above example, the circled numbers at the bottom refer to a string on which each note could be played. The other numbers refer to the fret on that string at which the note is to be found. The same note could be played on another string – so it is important to always refer to either the tablature or fingerboard diagram.

(3) Fingerboard diagram

Each horizontal line represents a string. The vertical lines represent the frets. Each fret is given a number in Roman numerals. Numbers on the horizontal lines indicate the left-hand finger to be used.

Play at the 3rd fret of the D string using the 3rd finger.

Guitarograph

All three previous methods are ways of illustrating the same information. In this book all are shown in combination, using the *guitarograph*. This leaves no doubt as to what is required.

This example therefore means:

        play string 3 at fret 3 (tablature),

        play the note C (notation),

        use finger 3 (fingerboard diagram).

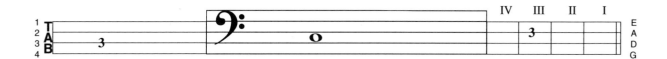

Above each *guitarograph* is an interval *formula*. This lists the letter names of the notes to be played, together with their *interval numbers*. The interval numbers refer to the position of the notes in comparison to the major scale of the same root.

For example:

C Major Scale

note names:	C	D	E	F	G	A	B	C
interval number:	R	2	3	4	5	6	7	R

C Major Arpeggio

note names:	C		E		G			C
interval number:	R		3		5			R

C Minor Arpeggio

note names:	C		E♭		G			C
interval number:	R		♭3		5			R

Octaves

The guitarographs on the following pages illustrate the chords that occur in the Grade Two musical examples. Notice that each arpeggio includes the root note twice. Once low (at the beginning of the arpeggio) and once high (at the end of the arpeggio). The high root note is known as the octave. This is a very useful note to include in your bass lines as it adds range and a sense of movement, and because it is simply the root note (but higher) it will always be in tune no matter what the type of chord.

G Major

G	B	D	G
R	3	5	R

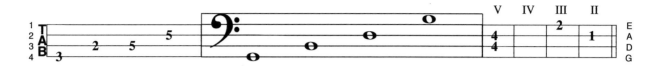

C Major

C	E	G	C
R	3	5	R

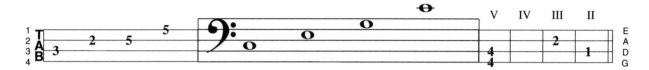

G Minor

G	B♭	D	G
R	♭3	5	R

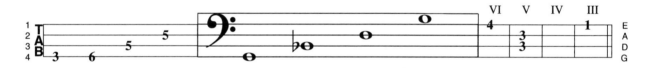

C Minor

C	E♭	G	C
R	♭3	5	R

G Major 7

G	B	D	F♯	G
R	3	5	7	R

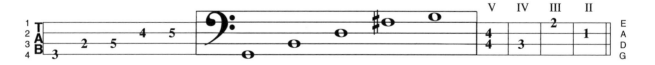

14

C Major 7

C	E	G	B	C
R	3	5	7	R

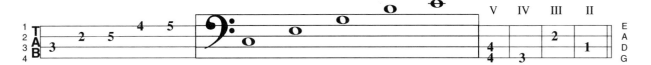

G Minor 7

G	B♭	D	F	G
R	♭3	5	♭7	R

C Minor 7

C	E♭	G	B♭	C
R	♭3	5	♭7	R

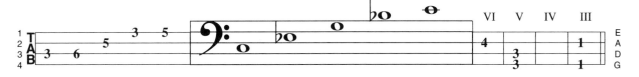

G 7

G	B	D	F	G
R	3	5	♭7	R

C 7

C	E	G	B♭	C
R	3	5	♭7	R

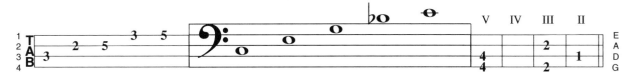

Using the CD, play along with the chord progressions below. Experiment by occasionally adding a seventh note to your improvisation. This will help you bring out the distinctive harmony of any seventh chords. At first you might like to establish a bass pattern that uses the root, third, fifth and (where appropriate) the seventh in a regular way. Once you become used to incorporating the seventh note, try and improvise a little more freely and vary the way that you use it on different chords. There is no need to play the seventh note on every seventh chord – how much use you make of the seventh note is really a matter of taste and what you think best suits the musical style. Attempting to use the root, third, fifth, seventh and octave over each chord would undoubtedly make your bass line sound too busy and over fussy. Sometimes the saying 'less is more' gives the best clue to establishing the right 'feel' for a piece of music. Before you begin to play, listen carefully to at least one verse of the backing track in order to choose an appropriate style of bass line.

Backing tracks

CD TRACK 10 – Country

| $\frac{4}{4}$ | G | Em | G | Em | Am | Am7 | D | D7 |

CD TRACK 11 – Romantic Ballad

| $\frac{3}{4}$ | A | AMaj7 | D | DMaj7 | C♯m | Bm7 | E | E7 |

CD TRACK 12 – Ska

| $\frac{4}{4}$ | C | Dm7 | Em7 | F | Am7 | G7 | C | C |

CD TRACK 13 – Jazz

| $\frac{4}{4}$ | G | E7 | A7 | A7 | D7 | D7 | G | D7 |